Nonprofit Startup Guide for Beginners

Easy Steps for Fundraising from
Small to Success

Table of Contents

Introduction

This book will help you in being able to start up your own nonprofit group from the ground up. Starting a nonprofit group is not easy and will require work, time, and patience from everyone involved. But, in the end, the work will be worth it because you will have started a business that will begin to impact your town, county, state, maybe even go as far as to impact people nationwide.

Everyone has heard of the big nonprofit organizations that are worldwide and reaching out to those that they help. The goal with this book is to give you the steps and help you get to that point. Everyone you are intending to help will, hopefully, get the help that you are wanting them to get!

Keep your mind open when going through this book in order to find out how to make your nonprofit business from start to finish. There are going to be some things that do not apply to your own nonprofit, and if that is the case, do not include them when starting your nonprofit. There are also going to be things that you are required to do that may seem to be making it harder for you to start your nonprofit, but that is not the case.

There are rules in place in order to keep nonprofits on the right track, make sure that you follow all the guidelines when it comes to any nonprofit business. It's not going to be easy to start up the nonprofit organization, but in the end, it will be worth it. Just make sure that you stick to your guns and don't give up.

This book will give you the basic tools that you need in order to start your own organization. All the work will come from you and take a lot of time, but with the right idea, you will be able to start a high-impact nonprofit organization that will be able to reach out to many.

CHAPTER ONE

What is a Nonprofit?

First of all, what you need to know is what a nonprofit is. A nonprofit is an organization that is established for other reasons other than to make a profit. It is usually started in order to advocate for a specific cause from a person(s) particular point of view. In other words, a nonprofit organization uses the revenue it receives to achieve their goals rather than spending the money on paying the shareholders of the organization.

The term nonprofit is used equally across the world so that everyone knows what the organization does. When it comes to accounting and legal purposes, there is a difference between a nonprofit organization and a not for profit organization. Just as there are differences between the nonprofit businesses and the for profit businesses.

Many people have come to associate nonprofit organizations as charitable organization. While this is true to a point. There are many other nonprofit organization sectors. A nonprofit overall is either a member serving or community severing organization. They are started to make an impact either with their members or within their communities.

Member serving organizations are started in order to serve a particular group of people. These organizations include things like credit unions, sports clubs, and retired serviceman's clubs. These organizations usually have membership fees that cover the costs of any of the organization.

Community serving organizations are there in order to serve the community around them or even started in order to make an impact globally. These organizations usually deliver human service programs that are things like medical care for those who can't afford it among other things.

The bottom line is a nonprofit is started to make an impact rather than to make a profit. Any money that enters into the nonprofit is used to help sustain the organization. Money can come from member dues as well as donations that come into the organization.

When starting your own organization, you need to decide on which of these nonprofits you want to start. A lot of nonprofits are community serving nonprofits that are in place to help serve the community around them (obviously).

Do not let this stop you though, if you are wanting to start a member serving nonprofit, then start one, and make sure that you follow all the guidelines that are in place for starting one. There may be a difference between what is required for having a community serving nonprofit versus a member serving one.

CHAPTER TWO

Research*

The very first thing that you have to do before you start your nonprofit is to do your research. What is it that you are trying to help? What is your cause? Do you want to be a community serving nonprofit or do you want to be a member serving organization? A big thing to remember is that a nonprofit is still a business like any other business. Your goals need to be realistic and obtainable. Starting a nonprofit is a lot like starting a for profit business. It has to have goals that you are able to keep in mind and reach as just stated. While you first start out in your progress, it is best to pretend that you already have the business and are making the decisions for a business that actually exists. It is a way for you to be able to see if the decisions that you make are worth making and going to actually make an impact or if they are going to harm your nonprofit. Write out all your goals and then even see if you can write out any pros and cons there would be to starting the nonprofit.

This would be kind of like writing out your business plan, but only you're writing out the goals that you want to obtain and you're also placing your ideas down on paper for you to actually see.

Here are some questions to ask yourself when doing your research.

- Is there a need for this kind of organization?

- Is there another organization already doing what I wish to do?

- Are my goals obtainable?

- What all do I need to have in order to start this organization?

- How quickly will this organization grow?

A good way to do this is to sit down and write your mission statement. What are you trying to achieve? Your mission statement should describe what it is you are trying to achieve. Essentially, the mission statement needs to answer this one big question.

Why does this organization exist?

The question is a tough one, but if you can answer that, then you are well on your way to starting up your own nonprofit organization. Again, if you can answer that and find that there are other organizations that already meet these needs, then perhaps you should think of joining them in their mission. This doesn't have to be a brand new idea either; you can take an idea that is already started and just place your own twist on it. For example, if you want to help children, then find something that is not being done to help out with the children.

While writing your mission statement, try and include values that will guide how your nonprofit will operate, primary benefits and services to clients, how you'd like others to view your nonprofit, and groups of clients who will benefit from these services. These should be included so that others know what the mission of your organization is as well as those that are working with you, know how to help you stick to your mission. This is important because you are going to live by your mission statement. This mission statement is going to be the entire object that you base your organization on. It is going to be how you make an impact.

Your mission statement doesn't have any specific length that it has to be. It can be anywhere from a few sentences to several pages. Just make sure that you are clear and concise about what it is that you want. Don't leave any room for any confusion. If there are parts that even you yourself are confused about, go back and rewrite your mission statement. Run your mission statement by other people to see if they are confused about anything. It is best to use simplified words so that your mission statement is easy to understand by all.

Another part of the research process is to figure out what kind of nonprofit you want to start. Do you just want it to be you and a few friends? Something like this would be something like starting a self-help group in your community. This type of nonprofit is called an informal nonprofit. The outreach is small but there is still an impact to those who are in need. Even in doing a small self-help group, there is the possibility that you are going to end up getting bigger than just one small self-help group. If you and your fellow nonprofit organization helpers are wanting to, you can start several self-help groups in different areas of your local area so that those who cannot travel as far will be able to attend the meetings if they really want to.

Do you want your nonprofit to continue after you're gone? If that is the case, then you may want to begin thinking of incorporating your nonprofit. In doing this, you are making sure that it exists as a separate legal organization. This ensures that it will continue that the nonprofit will continue on its own, have its own property as well as its own bank account, and will even protect you personally from liability. Just keep in mind that if you incorporate your nonprofit, you may be required to have a board of directors.

A board of directors is a group of people who will oversee the activities of your organization and help you make decisions. The board of directors is kind of like a sounding board. Instead of making any decisions on your own, you will have a group of people you are able to go to and get their opinion. In some organizations, the board of director makes the final decisions. If someone is no longer qualified to work for the organization, the board of directors will be the final group to decide if that individual is able to stay with the organization or is going to be terminated.

As with anything, there will be taxes. Talk to an accountant or the IRS to determine whether or not your nonprofit should be tax exempt or if it will qualify for tax deductions. Both of these statuses will depend on the nature of your organization as well as the services that are offered. If you work off of donations, there may be the possibility that you will be able to receive tax deductions for those donations.

Two last things that you need to research are, does your organization need a fiscal sponsor? And, do you need a lawyer? A fiscal sponsor will help get you started by sponsoring you because you don't have the sufficient resources to handle the startup costs and fees that come with starting a nonprofit organization. Not only will the help with the costs and fees associated with starting your organization, but they can help you gain the skills needed in order to manage the finances for your nonprofit.

Essentially, a sponsor is a more established nonprofit organization that will help you grow into the role of being a nonprofit. This is also called networking and the possibility that you and this other organization work together is going to be likely.

Do not take this organization for granted and go to them for everything. Learn things on your own so that you can make your own mistakes and learn from them. If you are unsure if the mistake is going to be detrimental to your organization, then you need to go to your fiscal sponsor and see what they think as well as consulting your board of directors.

Now that you've done all this work, you're going to want to protect it and yourself. A nonprofit lawyer will be able to help you with protecting all the hard work that you've put into starting your nonprofit. They'll be able to help you keep from being a for-profit organization as well as making sure all the forms are filled out properly for the IRS regarding tax exemptions and tax deductions. A lawyer will also be able to help you when it comes to setting up the organizations bank account, getting insurance for those that you hire, and how to make sure you are in line with the federal and state guidelines.

Any and all fees associated with starting up your own organization need to be paid. There is the possibility that your local or state government will have fees associated with you keeping your nonprofit open. This is where having a lawyer and accountant will come in handy. A lawyer will alert you of these fees and let you know what the money is going towards; while an accountant will help you to make sure that the fees get paid in order to keep your organization open.

An accountant will also be beneficial in making sure that you keep your nonprofits bank account in accordance with the guidelines that are required for you to follow. All receipts need to be kept for both income money and expenses. These will come in handy when it comes to doing taxes for your nonprofit organization.

CHAPTER THREE

Fundraising

You have started your nonprofit!! After all that research, you finally got the mission statement down, people who are going to work for you, a fiscal sponsor who is going to help you learn how to manage your finances and is going to help you with some of the startup costs. Not to mention you have turned in all your forms to the IRS after sending them to your lawyer and making sure that they were all in line with what is required for a nonprofit. At this point in time, you probably even have a board of directors that is there to help make sure you don't make any business decisions that could end up getting your organization closed. Everything seems good up to this point. But, where are you going to get money to keep your nonprofit running?

This is where fundraising comes into play. First of all, you need to decide what kind of fundraiser it is you want. One way is a event fundraiser. This can only be pulled off if you have a dedicated staff that you can trust so that you can delegate tasks out to certain members to be done. Event fundraisers are a great way to help get your fiscal sponsors involved as well as a great way to get the word out about your organization.

Event fundraisers involve getting donations of goods that you're going to auction off, supporters to help with entertainment, food, drinks, the event staff, the publicity, location, invitations, so on and so forth. All these are just part of what is needed in making sure that you have a successful event. Make sure that when you are planning an event, you are keeping your goals obtainable just as you did when you were first researching how to start your organization.

If this is your first event, keep it smaller so that you can see how it works out before making it a big event that everyone is sure to love. But, when starting with the smaller event, try out different ideas that you come up with to see if you can get donors or to see what your guests like and don't like. It is better to attempt to try out new ideas on a smaller group of people rather than to do something could cost you a lot more money in the end.

Another idea is to hold several small event fundraisers throughout the year that are set in place in advance so that the attendees know what to expect. Many attendees are repeaters because they believe in what the organization stands for and want to continue to share their support in some way, so they come to the events that are hosted by the nonprofit organization.

A big thing that you need to keep in mind with an event fundraiser is the timeline of the event. Don't put off any of the planning for last minute or else the fundraiser will not be as successful as you wish it to be. If you've picked a theme for your event, make sure that you don't have some obscure decorations that have nothing to do with the planned theme. Keep it all decent and possibly even simple. Don't put a negative view on your organization or it could be hard in the future.

If you do not have a large staff that you can delegate tasks out to or pay, you can also do a product fundraiser. These are good for clubs with members or church congregations. Consider the types of fundraisers that schools do, but with different products.

One good idea would be Auntie Anne's pretzels. Many people like Auntie Anne's and you can run a fundraiser like this for several weeks so that you can gain as many orders as possible. Don't limit it just to your local area either. Have your members reach out to their friends, family, co-workers, or anyone else who may be willing to help in making your fundraiser a success. A way that you can even reach out to the community is to set up a booth outside of a local supermarket that will allow you to sign up people willing to "donate" to your cause. If you do this though, make sure that you allow your customers to know that you will be back on a specific date and at a specific time so that they can pick up their goodies.

If you do not want to do food, you can also do a fundraiser using candles or any other various objects. Just make sure that you pick something that people are going to want to give money for. A good idea is to make sure that it is something that people buy year round and can even give as a gift. Many people use fundraisers as a way to shop for presents for birthdays, anniversaries, and holidays as well as being supportive of a charity or nonprofit organization. Make sure that anything you decide to do a fundraiser on is small and of good quality as well as being able to be affordable.

There will be costs associated with any fundraiser such as getting the items to the location and even paying the company in which the items are coming from, but the fees for these will not come out of your own pocket, they will work with you and their fees will be included in their price. The only thing that you need to make sure of is that you get enough orders for the price to possibly be lowered on the shipping and handling. Everyone has money difficulties. Keep in mind, would you want to spend that much on that object? If you wouldn't, then why have someone else do it?

Just like with anything, there are rules to being able to fundraise for a nonprofit organization. If you do not follow these rules, then there is a chance that your organization can be fined, you could lose your status as a nonprofit organization, or even closed down.

One of the first things that you need to do is to filled out a Unified Registration Statement (URS). This form is to help collect all the data that is required for any nonprofit that are performing charitable solicitations within their jurisdictions. If your state accepts the URS it can be used there as your registrations. Your nonprofit will be subject to the registration laws for any and all states that you are performing any charitable solicitations in. Some states have their own forms that are required that you will be required to fill out.

The few states that do not take the URS are: Florida, Oklahoma, and Colorado. In these states, you will be required to fill out the state forms. There is the possibility in these states that you will be required to write a check for any registration fees while adding in the proper forms and mailing them in to the administering agency. But, every other state uses the URS and if they do not, then they do not have any forms that need to be filled out. **But,** make sure that you get your local and state governments to tell you if they have any forms that need to be filled out. Do not just assume that there are no fees or forms to fill out because you live in a state that does not accept the URS. In doing this, you will be putting your organization in danger of being closed down.

Just like with anything there are certain rules that you must follow. When holding a fundraiser, you don't want to hire a firm to run your fundraiser for you because the firm will hold back some of the money in order to pay for all the expenses that they had to put out in order to deal with hosting the event. The percentage that goes to the firm that can be as high as 90% while only 10% of what actually comes in from the fundraiser will go to your cause.

How would you feel if you gave your to a nonprofit that you firmly believed in only to find out that a small percentage of your money is actually going to that organization? If you wouldn't tell your attendees about everything, then why do it?

The entire point for fundraising is to put money towards what your cause is, don't spend money on things that take money away from your cause. The whole purpose of starting your nonprofit organization was to bring your cause to a new light and to be able to make a change for your cause. This doesn't mean that you have to be cheap and make things look like they came from the dollar store, but that also doesn't mean that you have to go out and spend a ton of money on things that are necessary.

Basically, keep track of your spending because at the end of the year, you have to be able to show where all the money went that you spent. When doing the taxes in order to keep the tax exemption or tax deduction that your organization has gotten from the IRS. Every donation, every dollar that comes into the nonprofit has to be accounted for to make sure that you are not claiming a nonprofit status when you are actually a for-profit organization.

There is also the local business around your nonprofit that may be willing to donate to your organization. A lot of businesses actually have an amount set to the side that goes towards charitable giving. Some businesses can give more than others due to revenue, but they are always willing to try and help if it is within their budget. Even if they can no help financially, they almost always are willing to place fliers up for events that you may be having later on.

CHAPTER FOUR

Growing

S o now you've gone through all this trouble to start a nonprofit organization. You spent many man hours researching your cause and making sure that it was unique. After that, you spent all the time filling out paperwork and creating your organization. Then there was all the hours that you put in fundraising to make sure that your organization had enough money to stay afloat and reach out to the community and possibly even the entire nation (if that is the goal that you have). But, what is next?

Next comes getting out the word on your nonprofit. Even though you may have had an event fundraiser that brought some press in and probably got the news out about your organization. There is only so much fundraising you can do that your budget will allow. There is no possible way to continue to keep your organization in the press even though it would make getting the word out faster and easier, it can be too expensive for some nonprofits. Not to mention, you don't want to push your brand out to the community to the point that they become annoyed with you. There is a thin line between the right amount of media coverage and too much. It is a fine line that you will have to toe and make a decision on if you went overboard or not.

First, brand your organization. What are some of the biggest nonprofit organizations that come to mind? The red cross for the American

Red Cross, the black and white panda that represents WWF or even the blue hands that symbolize the Boys and Girls Club. Any of these nation-wide recognized symbols shows the view exactly what the cause is even without letting them know what the symbol stands for. Not to mention, there are constant commercials on television to constantly remind you that the organization is out there doing good for others.

Make your brand one that people can just see and instantly know what your cause is. There should be no question as to what you're trying to raise money and awareness for. Make sure that your brand has something to do with your cause as well. If you're trying to bring awareness to how many kids are falling behind in school because of their reading skills, don't pick a brand that could be misconstrued as having something to do with animals. This brand is going to be with the nonprofit organization for as long as the organization is going. Even as the years go on for your nonprofit, your brand may receive a facelift, but ultimately it will continue to stay the same because it is the brand that they know as yours.

Now that you have your own brand, get online! Everything now days is online. Everyone shops online, pays their bills online, and virtually lives online. With everyone always online, what is a better place to place your branding but online? There are various sites that will help you start your own website so that you have it set up in such a way that will give people access to finding out more about your organization and even donating online.

Also, reach out to the social media websites. Websites such as Facebook and Twitter are ways that you can use your brand and get the word out about your nonprofit. Appointing a social media expert is a good way to make sure that you can continue to have updates on your nonprofit set out for the public to see what is going on with your organization. With constant updates to your organization, you may find that followers of your nonprofit will help bring in more donors as well as volunteers for your nonprofit.

Not just will it bring in more sponsors or volunteers, but it will also gain more followers who also believe in your cause. There are always going to be more people out there in the world that believe in the same cause you do, but are not sure how to make an impact like you are planning to.

As I previously stated, you may have already had press coverage if you did an event fundraiser. Well, just because you can't constantly be in the media, doesn't mean that you can't continue to get some media coverage. Hopefully you've reached out and networked with several other nonprofit organizations and maybe made some media relationships. Use these relationships to your advantage.

Don't over use them to where it feels like you're just taking advantage of the person, but if you're having a fundraiser that maybe isn't as big, or you have some news that you want others to know about, use these contacts and get the word out! This is also beneficial if someone is attacking your organization. No one likes bad press, so get out there and show everyone that you're not what others may or may not be saying. You're here to support a good cause and everyone should know that. Or, if your cause is in desperate need of money or help, going back to my earlier example, you're trying to bring how many kids are left behind in school because of their reading skills, bring that to light. Get some volunteers to come out and help kids with reading difficulties. Get the community involved and have the media cover it to show just how your organization is trying to help out and make a difference.

Many media sources are willing to follow a nonprofit because they want to be there to get the story first when your organization makes the change that you want to make. Keep in mind, not all media representatives will want to get the story right. There will be people out there that want to bring you down, just push past them and keep your eye on your ultimate goal.

Yet another way that you can get the word out about your nonprofit is through mail. Registered mail sent through the post office goes out to everyone in the area and can give basic information about your nonprofit. You're not necessarily asking for money, you're just trying to get the community aware of what it is you're doing. This is a great way for people who are new to the area or other organizations to know about your nonprofit. This can result in more donations or volunteers if that is what you need. If the right person sees your registered mail, they may reach out to you telling you that they will be able to help you make your impact even bigger.

For example, if you are wanting to make an impact based on guidelines in schools based on how to help children who are falling behind due to reading skills, you may find that your registered mail reaches out to the superintendant of the school distract who has been worrying about the same thing.

Nonprofits more often times than not are organizations started by one or a group of people about a cause that bothers them but there are more people out there who are worried about the same cause but were not sure how to get their concern out or how to make an impact because they do not think that just they can make an impact.

As stated in the previous chapter, a lot of businesses are willing to place fliers up in their windows, in their break rooms, or on their bulletin boards to get people aware of any events that you may be having. In going along with this, place fliers in as many places as your community will allow. Some of the most unexpected places are actually the places that people look. If you are unsure of where you are allowed to place a flier, ask the business owner or your local police department if it is alright for a flier to be there.

If a flyer is too big to be placed somewhere, then go to something smaller such as a business card that states all your contact information and on the back, your mission statement or something similar that will let people know what your cause is.

Yet another way that word gets out about your nonprofit is through word of mouth. If your organization is one that helps people when a crisis hits their families, then when they come across someone who has hit a crisis in their life, they are going to tell them about you! Even if you can't do much in order to help them, a little goes a long way.

When you're out and about, you can always let others know about your nonprofit. Don't push it on someone who doesn't want to listen to what you have to say, but some people are more than willing to talk to you about your nonprofit and willing to listen not only because they may be in need of assistance, but because they want to make an impact as well. Without overdoing it, you may find little places in everyday conversations that you can slip in word about your nonprofit.

Make sure that those you do help (if that is what your organization does) know exactly what services you offer. These should have been placed in your mission statement that you created when you were doing your research in order to start your nonprofit in the first place. Not everyone is going to understand what your mission statement means, so make sure that you can simplify your mission statement into words that other people will be able to understand.

There are several opportunities to help your nonprofit grow; all that you have to do is to make sure that you take advantage of them. This is another great way to network with other nonprofits. If a nonprofit is unable to help someone due to how they have set up their mission statement or because they do not have the resources, they can always refer whoever is in need of help to your organization so that you may be able to help them instead.

Nonprofits are set up to make an impact even when it comes to helping out other nonprofit organizations. When they help another nonprofit, they are essentially helping themselves. It is much like the old saying, "I scratch your back, you scratch mine." If an organization helps you out by getting the word of your organization out, then you should do the same for them. This is a great way to keep your networking open and make good connections with the nonprofits in your area.

CHAPTER FIVE

Making an Impact

The whole reason that you wanted to start a nonprofit is so that you could make an impact either in your community, your state, or nationwide. In order to do that, you need to find some help. This ties into the last chapter where we talked about growing. In order to make an impact, you need to help your nonprofit grow. Networking is a big part of how this is going to go on. Network with other nonprofit organizations, local businesses, your local and state government, and even locations such as churches and the media so that you can get the furthest reach that you possibly can.

Just like we've already stated, a lot of businesses are willing to help with funding for nonprofits. But, a lot of companies do more than just help with the financial side of helping. A nonprofit is about reaching out and helping others. The biggest way to make an impact is to reach out through the businesses, your local government, other nonprofits, and even individuals in your community. Don't ever discount someone because you don't think that they will be able to help. Even the smallest help is going to help make an impact.

Ways to do this is to help with social media movements, volunteer with an event that they're hosting, or do whatever else is needed to help them. Some businesses will let you know if there is a special project that they need help with and they will let you know how they can use your help. This is not only good for you, but the business as well. You're both getting something that will help your own or even mutual cause.

When going through any local businesses, talk to the manager of that business to make sure that you are getting the appropriate information that you need in order to file out any paperwork there may be to see if you can get help from the business. While associates may have some of the information that you need, it is possible that the information they need is outdated. Any manger that speaks to you will give you the appropriate information and most likely even help you with filling out the paperwork to make sure that it is all filled out properly.

Do not assume that just because you fill out any paperwork involved with getting help from a business, that you will get it. Some of the larger businesses are constantly asked to help out from nonprofits and are unable to help everyone with whatever they have in their budget. Be patient while the manager takes the appropriate steps in order to see if you qualify for any help from them. There are no guarantees that you will get the help. The process of going through the applications and finding the right nonprofit can be tedious because the businesses have their own guidelines that they have to follow in order to accept the applications and give away the funds.

In the event that you get turned down for financial help from the local business, don't be discouraged, there are also government grants that can help. Local and state governments have scholarships set in place to help qualifying nonprofits. Look around online or go around your community to see who all has programs that may be willing to help you out. Churches are sometimes able to help based on their budget but also based on what your organization supports. Just like the local businesses, a church is not going to go against their religion or what their congregation would agree with.

Push the limits of what you think is possible. Think outside the box when it comes to the things that you can do. You started a nonprofit organization with the whole purpose of helping for the greater good. Even if your organization is based solely on focusing on one issue, that doesn't mean that you can't go out of your way to help with other things that will bring light to your organization.

Pick up trash along the side of the road with your organization and let your local or state government know that you're doing it in order to make sure that it is already first. If that is not something that you want to do, find something else in your community that needs to be done. Building playgrounds, helping repaint old buildings, stuff like that are great ways to take your nonprofit out and make a difference. In doing this, you don't have to wear clothing that will advertise your organization if that is not something that you want to do. People will know who did it because word will get out to the community.

Back to the picking up trash idea, you can also adopt a highway or a road and make the commitment to keep the stretch of road cleaned. Yes, a sign will go up that will say that that your organization has adopted the stretch of road, but it will also be a good way to get out word of your organization. People will drive down that stretch of road knowing that you made the commitment to keep it cleaned and see how well you keep your word. If you take on this responsibility, make sure that you are able to keep to a regular schedule of cleaning the stretch of road so that people can see how well you keep your word.

The biggest way to make an impact is to start by making an impact on the world around you. Start making an impact locally before you start trying to make an impact nationwide. As you work your way through your community, your dedication will get out and reach others who in turn will want to help you out with making an impact. The more people who want to help you make an impact, the bigger your reach will be.

It may not start right away, but the impacts will begin to be seen as time goes on. Don't get discouraged by any setbacks that may come your way. Every nonprofit will come across any setbacks and that is what helps them to overcome and adapt to whatever situation comes their way. There will be people who do not want to let you help make an impact and they will purposely make your life harder, but don't let that discourage you. Just keep on trucking and smile because you will make an impact in someone's life, even if it's just a smile.

CHAPTER SIX

Common Nonprofit Myths

Everything has myths. Myths are just common mistakes that people believe to be the truth. But, just as the word myth suggests, they are not true. The issues below do not determine if a nonprofit organization is successful or not. People will focus on the bad parts of an organization making others believe that the organization is not going to make a good impact because of these issues when in fact, some of the most successful nonprofits and even for-profits have these issues. The only difference between a nonprofit and a for profit is that a nonprofit doesn't focus on their issues, they focus on external good rather than internal structure.

1. There is no such thing as **perfect management**. Somewhere, everywhere, someone will mess up. But, just because someone does make a mistake, doesn't mean that the nonprofit can't be successful. If a manager or someone who is a position of power is making risks for the nonprofit, the board of directors can assign someone to help them correct their mistakes and place them on what would be considered a probationary period in which they are watched to make sure that their actions are corrected. If, this does not work, the manager can be replaced by someone who will reduce any of the risks that would put the organization in danger of losing their nonprofit status. This is another reason that many

nonprofit organizations share the leadership roles among several people, so that the leadership is not placed on just one person.

2. Yes, having a brand is important for your organization to be recognized, but, it isn't everything. Some of the major nonprofit organizations focus on marketing. The things that they do in their community have made their brand so well known that everyone can pick out what organization they are and what they do. This is called **brand-name awareness** which is why they don't have to market as much as some other organizations do. Even so, you can still market your organization to let others know what it is you do. Marketing is important, but not as important as making the impact that you want to make. Focus on making the impact and allow your brand to be known by the impact that you make. As you reach out and do good, people will begin to recognize your brand and what it is that you stand for.

3. You did all the research to make sure that you didn't make an organization that was similar to another organization. But, even if your organization is somewhat similar to another organization but differs, does not mean that it is a bad idea. There is no need to have a **breakthrough idea**. Taking an old idea and twisting it to where it is not you claiming someone else's idea, can actually make your nonprofit organization a success. The biggest thing that you need to remember is that you do not want to take someone else's idea and use it just as they did. Put your own spin on it because you never know what new ideas you might come up with. Just don't worry if you are unable to actually come up with

a brilliant, brand new idea because some ideas are going to be reused; only they are going to be rewritten so that an impact can be made.

4. You wrote your mission statement based on what *you* wanted your organization to accomplish. There is a possibility that you sat and wrote your mission statement out to where it is exactly what you want it to say, but chances are that you are too busy living out what your mission statement says and making an impact. There are no such things as **textbook mission statements**. Every organization has different mission statements that they live by. Very few organizations actually sit down and work on their mission statement with the exact verbage that will make it sound as if a lawyer wrote the statement. It is not necessary for your mission statement to use brilliant words that some people may not be able to pronounce or understand. The major thing is that your mission statement is something that you can live by and that you follow your mission statement because you wrote it out because it is something that you believe in.

5. All nonprofit organizations are measured based on how efficient they run. But, where whether you have **high rankings on the conventional metrics** on the rating scale or not, it does not determine how big of an impact you make. The biggest reason that most nonprofits don't score well on the conventional metrics is because of how misleading the metrics are because of the things that they measure. Overhead rations do not always apply to nonprofit organizations because they are too busy trying to make an

impact. Your ranking on the conventional metrics scale is only going to show where you sit financially amongst the other non-profit organizations. This does not mean that you are not making an impact; especially if you just started out.

6. Some nonprofit organizations have very **large budgets** that they are able to work with when trying to make an impact while others do not have a large budget. Does money make an impact when trying to change the world? It can, but it is not everything. If you are just trying to reach out to people and let them know that they are not allow, then that does not take money to do. Large budget to no budget, it doesn't matter how much money you spend, all that matters is that you reach your goal and stay committed to your goals. Continue to follow the mission statement that you first made out when you first started your organization. It is the cause that matters the most, not the amount of money that you spend on trying to make a difference.

CHAPTER SEVEN

Six Practices of High-Impact Nonprofits

In the world of nonprofit organizations, the secret to success is to be a force for good. To be a high impact nonprofit you have to work outside the boundaries of your organization instead of worrying about how to manage your internal operations. Most organizations are satisfied with an organization that is just good enough while focusing all their energy externally to make a change on a larger scale. Nothing matters more than to be able to make a difference when that was what you started out to do in the first place.

To quote Archimedes, "Give me a lever long enough and I alone can move the world." In other words, one person alone can change the world if they have enough ambition. But, even in that, it requires a small initial investment that was invested in your organization when you first started your nonprofit. With that small initial investment you can gain a high return using your leverage the right way in order to make a change.

1. To go back to the previous example earlier, if your organization is set out to help kids who are falling behind in school because of their reading skills, you've probably got volunteers that are helping kids with their reading skills so that they aren't falling behind in school as much. You're **serving** your community when you send out volunteers to help with this issue. But, service only

goes so far, you also need to **advocate** for your cause. Have the businesses that you work with help you change the practices in schools by having teachers become more aware of the issue and to have them helping the children who are falling behind and begin helping the children. Use whatever networking you have to advocate what your cause is. Sometimes businesses can change their policy to help make an impact, or local/state government can change laws or even make laws that are going to help you with making an impact for your cause. It won't be an overnight impact, but it will be something you'll be able to follow through with and see the change as it happens.

2.   The businesses that you work with are there to help you make a change in all the different ways that you are needing help. Use the businesses that you work with and **make the market work** in your favor. For example, when the Environmental Defense worked with McDonalds, they make the packing more environmentally sound. The biggest way that the make the market work is to help change business practices on a larger scale.

3.   Volunteers, donors, and advisers are highly appreciated for the time that they put into the organization, but also for the **evangelism** that they provide for the nonprofit. In turn for making a connection with the nonprofit on an emotional level, they turn around and get more supporters for the nonprofit that they work with. In doing this they use viral marketing as well as other ways in order to spread the word about the nonprofit.

4. Just like when you were fundraising or trying to get media support in order to spread the word about your nonprofit. The other thing to do is to make sure that you **nurture any networks** that you have been able to make. Instead of trying to tear down their competitors, they help build up their peers by sharing the information that they get in advancing in their specific fields as far as wealth, expertise, talent and power. They do this not because they are saints, but because it is in their best interest to do so.

5. With times constantly changing, nonprofits and for-profits are being forced to change to adapt with the times. This has made high-impact nonprofits the **masters of adaptation**. In order to adapt to the times that are changing, they change their tactics in order increase the success of their organizations. Even in doing so, they are forced to change their strategies and learn from their mistakes in order to keep up with everything that is going on. This means that the nonprofit has to master the ability to listen, modify, and learn from the external cues that others give them.

6. The biggest success for any high impact nonprofit is to **share leadership.** Egos in some for-profits have an oversized ego because they are able to solely make the decisions and when something goes right, they get all the credit for what has gone right. But, with a nonprofit, they share the leadership responsibilities in order to be a stronger force for good. By distributing the leadership within their organization as well as within their external nonprofit networks to cultivate a strong leadership team. They

are able to listen to the various ideas that others have and implement them if they are going to help their cause. Just because one person comes up with an idea, does not mean that it cannot be changed up by someone else to make the idea even stronger.

All these are what makes a nonprofit organization high impact. Just remember to keep your networks open and share the ideas that you come up with in order to help make other nonprofits just as impactful as yours.

CHAPTER EIGHT

Helpful Resources

Just as a quick rundown of everything that we've talked about, this chapter will give you some helpful resources and condensed versions of what has already been stated in this book. All these resources are meant to help you in starting your nonprofit and keeping it going while making a big impact on those around you, bringing light to a cause that you find worthy of bringing a light to and helping you reach your full potential as a nonprofit.

Nonprofit checklist:

1. Pick a name. Words like Inc. Lt. and Corp are helpful in identifying who you are. If you are unsure which one to pick, go online and see which one would be best for you.

2. Make sure that your name is not already taken or similarly taken. You want to be unique.

3. Get whatever name you pick registered so that it belongs to you and no one can take it as you begin the buildup of your nonprofit.

4. Decide where you want your nonprofit to be based out of or incorporated. Many nonprofits and even regular businesses are incorporated in the home state of which they are started.

5. Choose your board of directors. Your board of directors will help in making important decisions based on what needs to happen with your nonprofit. They will also be the ones who are responsible for helping you decide how to invest money in order to grow your nonprofit.

6. Create your nonprofits articles of incorporation or in other words, the corporate charter. This is basically a piece of paper that is stating that you exist as a nonprofit organization.

7. Along with creating the articles of incorporation, you need to file them with your secretary of state and pay all the filing fees.

8. Create your by-laws. These are rules established for your organization to regulate itself.

9. Next comes your tax exemption status as well as the tax deductions. Apply for all statuses that your organization is eligible for with both the federal and state governments.

10. Now get your nonprofit business permits and licenses. You'll need to do this on all three government levels. Make sure you register with your local government, state, and then the federal government. Also, make sure to follow all rules and guidelines set forth by these governments as they pertain to your organization.

11. There is no doubt that you'll be getting donations that will help you with the impact of your nonprofit, open a bank account that will be strictly for the nonprofit organization. This bank account

will have records of where all the money came into your organization as well as where it went out and for what.

12. To make sure that all your paperwork is in order and stays in order, hire a lawyer that will make sure everything is properly filled out and filed. A lawyer will also be there in case of more extreme circumstances should they arise.

This website is a PDF form that will give you many resources in helping you start your organization and make sure that you follow all the appropriate guidelines.

www.ag.state.mn.us/Charity/Forms/*NonProfitResources*.pdf

This website is a website that answers some of the most commonly asked questions when it comes to nonprofits. It answers questions such as, what is a nonprofit, as well as where the money for the nonprofit comes from.

http://www.idealist.org/info/Nonprofits

Disclaimer

All the information in this book was collected and compiled in a way that would help start a nonprofit organization. None of the forms that are required to start a nonprofit are included in this book and all information is a generic version of what needs to be done.

Make sure that you contact your local government as well as your state government to get all the appropriate forms to fill out and establish your organization. Also make sure to follow all the guidelines that are required by these governments in order to make sure that your nonprofit is legal on all aspects.

As it may be, there is a possibility of fees coming up after you have filed all your paperwork and have started your organization. Make sure to pay all these fees in order to keep your nonprofit going.

Any questions that weren't answered in this book can be found either online or by going to your local government and asking them any questions that you have. If you are unsure if you want to start your own nonprofit, volunteer at a local nonprofit organization and see what it is like to make an impact. Get in contact with the director and see if there is any way that you might be able to look into their internal structure and how things are set up within their organization.

Remember to always be courteous when talking to someone who runs a business and that they may say no to giving you intimate details about how their organization works. If this is the case, see if they would sit down with you and offer you some advice in how to start your own organization. As stated in this book, many nonprofit organizations are going to help those around them in order to help make them successful as well because it is part of reaching out towards their community.

Any impact you make may not be made overnight, but it will be something that you can follow through with and watch as it makes the impact that you want. The best part is that you will know that you were part of what made the change. Any impact you make will make you feel good because you will know that you helped change history. Especially when you are able to follow the impact from start to finish.

All nonprofits are started to help make the impact that everyone wants to make, but no one knows how to do. All it takes is for one person to be brave enough to step up and start trying to change lives one day at a time. It is never easy for someone to be brave enough to say that things need to change, but as more and more people see that they are not alone in their beliefs, they will stand up and help you make an impact as well.

Sometimes the simplest way to make an impact on someone is to just smile, or offer a kind word to them. It may not be what your cause is, but it is something that will begin to make an impact on others. If you can make that impact, then you are going to be able to make a change with your organization.

Conclusion

Thank you again for downloading this book!

I hope this book was able to help you to start your nonprofit organization and give you some ideas on how to fundraise, make a change, and grow your nonprofit organization from the ground up. It won't be easy, but it will be something that will more than be worth your time.

The next step is to get out there, start your nonprofit, and start making the impact that you want to make. Just remember that some things in this book may differ in your state from what has been stated in this book.

Finally, if you enjoyed this book, please take the time to share your thoughts and post a review on Amazon. It'd be greatly appreciated!

Thank you and good luck!